Cookies

fun and tasty treats

Yasa Boga

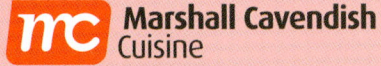
Marshall Cavendish Cuisine

Translation by Ilona Pitt
Design by Steven Tan
Photographs by Soerjanto Photography

Published by Marshall Cavendish Cuisine
An imprint of Marshall Cavendish International

Other Marshall Cavendish Offices:
Marshall Cavendish International. PO Box 65829, London, EC1P 1NY, UK • Marshall
Cavendish Corporation, 99 White Plains Road, Tarrytown NY 10591-9001, USA •
Marshall Cavendish International (Thailand) Co Ltd. 253 Asoke, 12th Flr, Sukhumvit
21 Road, Klongtoey Nua, Wattana, Bangkok 10110, Thailand • Marshall Cavendish
(Malaysia) Sdn Bhd, Times Subang, Lot 46, Subang Hi-Tech Industrial Park, Batu Tiga,
40000 Shah Alam, Selangor Darul Ehsan, Malaysia

Marshall Cavendish is a trademark of Times Publishing Limited

National Library Board, Singapore Cataloguing-in-Publication Data

Yasa Boga (Group)
Cookies : fun and tasty treats / Yasa Boga. Singapore: Marshall Cavendish Cuisine,
c2010.
p. cm. (Home cooking)
ISBN-13 : 978-981-4302-28-9

1. Cookies. I. Title. II. Series: Home cooking.

TX772
641.8654 – dc22   OCN639727733

Printed in Malaysia by Times Offset (M) Sdn Bhd

contents

introduction

Baking cookies is relatively simple compared to baking cakes, as it does not require special techniques or specific utensils. The worst that can happen would be getting burnt cookies, cookies which are not as crunchy as they should be, or cookies which are too chewy or hard from over-kneading. In general, the cookies would still have a fine aroma and taste delicious regardless of its texture.

Making cookies require careful planning and preparation in order to yield better results. A perfect batch of cookies will have the following attributes: uniformity in colour and size, the right level of sweetness, saltiness or a rich flavour, a distinctive aroma, crunchiness and crispness. To achieve the best results, take note of some tried-and-tested techniques and pointers in this section.

Essentially, all cookie recipes require the following basic ingredients—butter, sugar, flour, and eggs. Cookies can be classified by the different textures of cookie dough and varying cookie shapes.

types of cookies

Bar Cookies

Due to their soft texture, the dough for bar cookies needs to be rolled out directly in the baking tray or tin that the cookie dough will set or be baked in. Grease and line the tin or baking tray with non-stick baking paper. Transfer the dough into the tin or tray and cover it with another sheet of non-stick baking paper. Use the back of a metal spoon or a small rolling pin to roll out and press the top of the baking paper. Spread the dough out evenly such that the mixture fills up the entire tin or tray. Ensure that the dough is not spread out too thin; otherwise, the cookies would be hard and dry. Similarly, if the mixture is too thick, the cookies may turn out unevenly baked.

If the dough requires baking, you can either score the dough to the desired shape and size with a sharp knife before baking, or remove the dough from the oven when it is three-quarters cooked as specified in individual recipes, then score it before returning it into the oven to continue baking.

Rolled/Cut-out Cookies

A touch firmer than bar cookies, the dough for rolled or cut-out cookies should also be placed on a baking tray lined with non-stick baking paper or cling film. Cover the dough with another sheet of non-stick baking paper before rolling it out to a thickness of 0.5-cm ($^1/_4$-in) with a rolling pin. Various cookie shapes can be cut out with cookie cutters made from tin, stainless steel or plastic.

Besides cut-out cookies, there are some cookies where the dough is shaped in carved wooden moulds, such as *spekulaas*. The dough is packed into individual moulds and any excess dough is scraped with a knife. By tapping on the moulds, the cookies are unmoulded and placed on a baking tray before baking.

If you are making cut-out cookies which are rather thick and big in size, it can be difficult to transfer the cookie shapes onto a baking tray as they may fall apart. For easy handling, roll out the dough in a baking tin or tray lined with non-stick baking paper, then use a cookie cutter of choice to cut the dough into shapes. Space the cookies out on the baking tray. Remove the remaining dough around the edges of each cut-out cookie with a blunt knife or spatula. Transfer the baking paper with the cookies on top directly onto a baking tray before putting it in the oven.

Piped/Pressed Cookies

The cookie doughs for piped/pressed cookies come in varying degrees of softness. Some pressed cookies can be shaped with a special utensil called a *spuit*.

cookies can be shaped with a special utensil called a *spuit*. Generally, this utensil is cylindrical and made of plastic or metal. It resembles and works like a giant syringe. The cookie dough is put into the utensil and piped onto the baking tray, forming shapes according to the design or pattern of the nozzle attached to the utensil.

Some recipes for pressed cookies that yield an exceedingly soft dough are not suitable for being shaped with a *spuit* because the dough may stick to the insides of the cylinder and not be piped out properly. In cases like this, use a piping bag attached with a plastic or metal nozzle to pipe cookies out.

When making pressed cookies, it is important to note that the cookie dough should be piped directly onto ungreased, chilled baking trays (this will help the cookies retain their shape and not melt before baking).

No-bake Cookies
The cookies in this category usually contain a lot of chocolate, as it helps to set and hold the dough together when chilled. After shaping, the cookie mixture is simply left to set before being stored in airtight containers and refrigerated.

Drop Cookies
As implied by its name, the cookies in this category are formed by dropping teaspoonfuls of relatively soft dough onto a baking tray. You can easily do this by using a teaspoon to scoop the cookie dough and another teaspoon to shape the dough a little before 'dropping' the dough onto the baking tray.

Moulded Cookies
Moulded cookies are made from slightly stiff but still pliable dough that are moulded into different shapes using your hands. Some common shapes include small balls, plaits or even a cylinder, which is sliced into thin rounds.

basic ingredients

Butter/Margarine
Made from milk, butter enriches the flavour and aroma of cookies. Canned butter, which is salty, cultured and has the aroma of cheese can be used, but only in certain recipes where its flavour will be enhanced by the ingredients.

Margarine is also salty in flavour. Several recipes in this book include margarine for the sole purpose of ensuring that the cookies will taste light and not turn out brittle. Regardless of whether you are using unsalted butter, salted butter or margarine, always add salt, if you are using any, after the butter, sugar and eggs have been well combined, as it accentuates the rich flavours of the cookies. To estimate how much salt to add, taste a little of the cookie mixture before adding any salt.

Flour

Unless specified otherwise, always use plain flour. As flour may absorb moisture in humid conditions, it is advisable to sun-dry the flour for 1-3 hours, or to dry-fry it quickly in a frying pan for about 5 minutes over low heat. After frying, sift flour for 2–3 times before use. This process ensures that all the flour granules are loosened, which gives cookies a crisp, crunchy texture.

Sugar

Ideally, use castor (superfine) sugar as it has smaller granules. Icing (confectioner's) sugar can be used as a substitute, provided it has been sifted 2–3 times to ensure that the sugar granules are loosened and separated.

Eggs

Fresh eggs are essential, especially for recipes that require the use of egg whites, as aged egg whites do not coagulate well. Always use eggs at room temperature. Cold eggs will cause the cookie batter to lose its air cells and result in cookies which are dry and flat in texture. Egg whites at room temperature will also foam quickly, and achieve a greater volume when whipped.

additional ingredients

Candied Fruit

An example of candied fruits would be glacé cherries which are sold soaked in sugar syrup. Dab dry with paper towels before use.

Nuts

Dry-fry nuts briefly until they are lightly toasted and fragrant, or dry-roast them in the oven. Chop them according to the instructions in the recipe.

Spices

Ready-to-use ground spices are easily available. However, you can prepare them yourself by grinding the whole seeds in a mortar and pestle, and dry-frying the powder until fragrant. Store ground spices in airtight containers or bottles to retain their aromas and flavours.

Vanilla Extract

Vanilla extract has a stronger and less artificial flavour compared to vanilla essence. Despite being more expensive, a bit of vanilla extract goes a long way.

baking equipment

You do not need top-of-the-range equipment to make cookies. Essentially, you need: weighing scale, mixing bowls, an electric mixer, baking paper, plastic wrap, a wooden spoon or rubber spatula, a flat metal spatula, baking tins or trays, and wire racks.

Additional equipment such as a wooden rolling pin, piping bag and serrated nozzles, cookie cutters or wooden moulds are needed for rolled and pressed cookies, or as specified in the recipes.

baking techniques

Sifting

Mix and sift together all ingredients in powder form (such as flour, cocoa powder, ground cinnamon) until well combined at least twice.

Beating

Beat the butter, sugar and eggs until the mixture is doubled in volume, and is thick and pale in colour. Do not over-beat the mixture, as it will cause the cookies to expand too much when baked, and the butter to liquefy and separate. If this happens, refrigerate the mixture for a while before beating it again until it is creamy. Beat the butter and sugar until the mixture is fluffy, and use a wooden spoon to stir in the eggs a little at a time. Do not stir for too long as this will result in too much air being trapped in the batter.

Forming the Cookie Batter

Add flour to the liquid mixture in small batches, stirring gently with a wooden spoon or fork until well-combined and not sticky to the touch. If kneading by hand, do this as quickly as possible as butter melts easily and will cause the cookies to be less crunchy when baked.

Additional dry ingredients such as nuts, dried fruits and candied fruits are usually added to the batter at the end.

Rolling Out/Shaping Cookie Dough

It is best to place the cookie dough between two sheets of baking paper or plastic wrap, and use a wooden rolling pin to gently roll out the dough. Start from the centre of the dough to the edges and roll it to a 0.5-cm ($^{1}/_{4}$-in) thickness. Do not press or roll too hard, as this will cause the dough to compact excessively, resulting in hard cookies.

Before cutting out cookie shapes, dip the cookie cutter in some flour to prevent the dough from sticking to the cutter. Likewise, if using a wooden mould (when making *spekulaas*), sprinkle some flour particularly in the carved crevices. Tap the mould to ensure that all parts of the mould are equally and lightly coated in flour, and shake off the excess.

If the cookie dough for rolled and moulded cookies is too sticky to roll out or to shape, wrap in plastic wrap and store in the refrigerator for 10–15 minutes to allow the mixture to set again before shaping. The cookie mixture can also be made in advance and stored in the refrigerator a few days before baking.

Baking

When baking cookies, choose baking trays with non-shiny surfaces such as tin trays. Shiny metals absorb more heat and will cause the cookies to bake too quickly. Take note of whether the tray should be greased or not, as specified in the recipe.

Preheat oven to the temperature specified in the recipe for about 10 minutes before baking. It is not advisable to leave rolled/cut-out cookies in the open for too long.

Space the cookies out on the baking tray as specified in the recipes to prevent them from sticking together when they expand during baking.

Always place the baking tray on the middle shelf to ensure even baking. However, if you intend to place more trays on the top and bottom shelves, rotate them midway through baking to allow cookies to be evenly baked.

After baking for approximately 15–25 minutes, the cookies will turn brown and have crisp edges, which means they are done. Remove them from the oven and leave them to cool and set. However, cookies made from a cookie dough that is chilled in the fridge prior to shaping will require a longer time to set.

decorating tips

Sprinkling/Pasting

Sprinkle chopped nuts, fruits or other decorations over the cut/moulded cookie shapes, as specified in the recipes. Use the tip of a chopstick or a tiny rolling pin and gently press in the decorations so they will not fall out after the cookies are done.

Frosting

Apply frosting only after the cookies have cooled and set. Cut off the tip of a piping bag and attach a nozzle of choice. Transfer the sugar frosting into the piping bag and knot the open end. Pipe frosting onto each cookie and decorate as desired.
A blunt knife can be used to spread an even layer of sugar frosting on each cookie.

Sugar Frosting
1 egg white 250 g (9 oz)
Icing (confectioner's) sugar
1–2 tsp lime/lemon juice/white vinegar (add extra if the mixture is still too thick for piping)

• Beat egg white in a bowl with an electric mixer. Add icing (confectioner's) sugar a little at a time while beating continuously. Finally, stir in juice or vinegar and beat until very stiff peaks form. You may add a few drops of food colouring and essence of choice into the mixture. The frosting should be a creamy paste that can be piped onto the cookies.

Chocolate Dip
100 g (3$^1/_2$ oz) cooking chocolate + $^1/_2$ tsp butter

• Combine cooking chocolate and butter in a small heatproof bowl. Melt the chocolate mixture in the microwave or use a double boiler. If you do not have a double boiler, place the chopped pieces of chocolate in a bowl that can sit on the top of a saucepan of simmering water without the bottom of the bowl touching the water. Stir until the chocolate has melted completely.

If you intend to pipe the chocolate mixture onto your cookies, place the chocolate pieces and butter into a piping bag, knot the open end of the bag and immerse it in a saucepan of water over low heat. Continue heating until the chocolate melts. Remove and leave the mixture to cool before piping onto cookies.

 storing

Before storing, allow cookies to cool completely on a wire rack, unless specified otherwise. Store cookies in airtight containers in a cool, dry place for maximum freshness. Most cookies should stay crunchy and retain their taste and aroma for up to one month. Place silica gel bags into the containers to further protect cookies from humidity.

weights and measures

Quantities for this book are given in Metric, Imperial and American (spoon) measures. Standard spoon and cup measurements used are: 1 tsp = 5 ml, 1 Tbsp = 15 ml, 1 cup = 250 ml. All measures are level unless otherwise stated.

LIQUID AND VOLUME MEASURES

Metric	Imperial	American
5 ml	$1/6$ fl oz	1 teaspoon
10 ml	$1/3$ fl oz	1 dessertspoon
15 ml	$1/2$ fl oz	1 tablespoon
60 ml	2 fl oz	$1/4$ cup (4 tablespoons)
85 ml	$2^1/2$ fl oz	$1/4$ cup
90 ml	3 fl oz	$3/8$ cup (6 tablespoons)
125 ml	4 fl oz	$1/2$ cup
180 ml	6 fl oz	$3/4$ cup
250 ml	8 fl oz	1 cup
300 ml	10 fl oz ($1/2$ pint)	$1^1/4$ cups
375 ml	12 fl oz	$1^1/2$ cups
435 ml	14 fl oz	$1^3/4$ cups
500 ml	16 fl oz	2 cups
625 ml	20 fl oz (1 pint)	$2^1/2$ cups
750 ml	24 fl oz ($1^1/5$ pints)	3 cups
1 litre	32 fl oz ($1^3/5$ pints)	4 cups
1.25 litres	40 fl oz (2 pints)	5 cups
1.5 litres	48 fl oz ($2^2/5$ pints)	6 cups
2.5 litres	80 fl oz (4 pints)	10 cups

DRY MEASURES

Metric	Imperial
30 grams	1 ounce
45 grams	$1^1/2$ ounces
55 grams	2 ounces
70 grams	$2^1/2$ ounces
85 grams	3 ounces
100 grams	$3^1/2$ ounces
110 grams	4 ounces
125 grams	$4^1/2$ ounces
140 grams	5 ounces
280 grams	10 ounces
450 grams	16 ounces (1 pound)
500 grams	1 pound, $1^1/2$ ounces
700 grams	$1^1/2$ pounds
800 grams	$1^3/4$ pounds
1 kilogram	2 pounds, 3 ounces
1.5 kilograms	3 pounds, $4^1/2$ ounces
2 kilograms	4 pounds, 6 ounces

OVEN TEMPERATURE

	°C	°F	Gas Regulo
Very slow	120	250	1
Slow	150	300	2
Moderately slow	160	325	3
Moderate	180	350	4
Moderately hot	190/200	370/400	5/6
Hot	210/220	410/440	6/7
Very hot	230	450	8
Super hot	250/290	475/550	9/10

LENGTH

Metric	Imperial
0.5 cm	$1/4$ inch
1 cm	$1/2$ inch
1.5 cm	$3/4$ inch
2.5 cm	1 inch

cereal bar

125 g (4$^{1}/_{2}$ oz) dark cooking chocolate, melted

85 g (3 oz) raisins, roughly chopped

75 g (2$^{2}/_{3}$ oz) walnuts or pecans or dry-roasted cashew nuts, coarsely chopped

80 g (2$^{4}/_{5}$ oz) castor (superfine) sugar

90 g (3$^{1}/_{4}$ oz) unsalted butter + more for greasing

1$^{1}/_{4}$ tsp salt

50 g (1$^{2}/_{3}$ oz) red and green glacé cherries, chopped

40 g (1$^{1}/_{3}$ oz) cornflakes, lightly crumbed

45 g (1$^{1}/_{2}$ oz) desiccated coconut

- Prepare a 30 x 10-cm (12 x 4-in) baking tin. Line with aluminium foil and grease with butter.
- Pour melted chocolate into tin to form an even layer. Set aside.
- In a medium-size pot, cook raisins, nuts of choice, sugar, butter and salt over low heat until sugar has dissolved and butter has melted.
- Add cherries, cornflakes and desiccated coconut. Stir to mix well.
- Remove mixture from heat and immediately transfer to prepared tin. Working quickly, press mixture with the back of a fork to form an even, compact layer over chocolate layer.
- Chill in fridge until set. Cut and serve as desired.

NOTE:

This cereal bar requires no baking. It contains a lot of chocolate to hold the ingredients together and therefore needs to be set in the fridge before cutting. Store the cereal bars in airtight containers in the fridge.

janhagels

300 g (11 oz) butter

175 g (6^1/$_4$ oz) icing (confectioner's) sugar

2 egg yolks

350 g (12 oz) plain (all-purpose) flour

100 g (3^1/$_2$ oz) blanched almonds,
coarsely chopped

100 g (3^1/$_2$ oz) castor (superfine) sugar
for sprinkling

Glaze

2 egg yolks, whisked with 1 tsp melted butter

- Preheat oven to 160°C (325°F). Prepare two 25-cm (10-in) square baking trays. Line trays with baking paper. Set aside.

- With an electric mixer, beat butter, icing sugar and egg yolks until light and fluffy. Add flour to mixture and stir in flour with a fork or wooden spoon until combined and dough no longer feels sticky to touch.

- Divide dough into 2 equal portions and place on baking trays. Cover with plastic wrap or a sheet of non-stick baking paper. With a rolling pin, roll out dough on tray to a thickness of 0.5-cm (^{1}/$_4$-in). Remove plastic wrap or baking paper and brush surface of dough with egg yolk glaze. Sprinkle almonds and sugar over dough.

- Place trays in preheated oven and bake for 15–20 minutes. Remove trays and immediately cut each sheet of dough into 5 x 2^1/$_2$-cm (2 x 1-in) pieces with a sharp knife. Return to oven and bake for about 5 minutes until golden brown.

- Remove and leave to cool before serving or storing in airtight containers.

scottishshortbread

180 g (6$^1/_2$ oz) butter

40 g (1$^1/_3$ oz) icing (confectioner's) sugar

1 tsp lemon zest

230 g (8$^1/_4$ oz) plain (all-purpose) flour
+ 30 g (1 oz) rice flour, sifted

- Preheat oven to 170°C (330°F). Prepare 2 baking trays. Line trays with baking paper. Set aside.

- With an electric mixer, beat butter, icing sugar and lemon zest until light and fluffy. Stir in flour mixture with a fork or wooden spoon until combined and dough no longer feels sticky to touch.

- Divide dough into 4 equal portions. With a rolling pin, roll out each portion of dough between 2 sheets of plastic wrap to a thickness of about 0.5-cm ($^1/_4$-in).

- Cut out 4 round shapes with a 20-cm (8-in) diameter round cake ring. Using 1 end of a chopstick, make creases around edges of each dough circle. Score the top of each dough circle into 8 equal wedges and prick each wedge with a fork to create a pattern. Transfer dough to baking trays.

- Bake on bottom shelf of preheated oven for about 25 minutes until dough circles are almost cooked. Remove trays from oven and cut each dough circle along score marks into neat wedges. Return trays to middle shelf of oven and bake for about 10 minutes until golden brown.

- Remove and leave to cool before serving or storing in airtight containers.

checkers

240 g (8²/₃ oz) unsalted butter

³/₄ tsp salt

400 g (14¹/₃ oz) plain (all-purpose) flour

150 g (5¹/₃ oz) icing (confectioner's) sugar

1 egg

1 tsp vanilla extract or ¹/₄ tsp ground vanilla

2 tsp cocoa powder or more, if required

1 egg white

* In a large mixing bowl, add butter, salt, flour and sugar and mix with a wooden spoon until mixture is grainy. Add egg and vanilla. Stir to mix well.

* For version A cookies, divide dough into 2 equal portions. Add cocoa powder to 1 portion and mix well to form chocolate dough. Use a rolling pin to roll out both portions of dough to similar rectangular shapes with a thickness of 1-cm (¹/₂-in). Wrap dough separately with baking paper and chill in fridge.

* Preheat oven to 170°C (330°F) while dough is chilling.

* To make version A cookies, remove chilled dough from fridge. Cut each rectangular shape along its length into 3 equal blocks. Arrange blocks of dough together to form a checkered pattern (see diagram). Brush egg white along the sides of each block to glue and set dough. Wrap dough in baking paper and return to fridge to chill until set.

* When chilled, remove combined block of dough from fridge and slice along its breadth into 0.5-cm (¹/₄-in) thick slices. Arrange cookies on lined baking trays. Bake for 20–25 minutes until cookies are done.

* For version B cookies, divide dough into 3 equal portions. Add 2 tsp cocoa powder to 2 portions of dough and mix well to form chocolate dough. Divide chocolate dough back into 2 equal portions. Use a rolling pin to roll out the 3 portions of dough to similar rectangular shapes with a thickness of 1-cm (¹/₂-in). Wrap dough separately with baking paper and chill in fridge.

* To make version B cookies, cut plain dough and 1 portion chocolate dough along its length into 2 equal blocks (see diagram). Arrange blocks of dough together to form a checkered pattern. Brush egg white along the sides of each block to glue and set dough. Wrap dough in baking paper and return to fridge to chill until set.

- When chilled, remove combined block of checkered dough from fridge. Roll out remaining portion of chocolate dough to a rectangular sheet with sufficient width and length to wrap around the block of checkered dough.

- Chill briefly before slicing along its breadth into 0.5-cm (¹/₄-in) thick slices. Bake for 20–25 minutes until cookies are done. Remove and leave to cool before serving or storing in airtight containers.

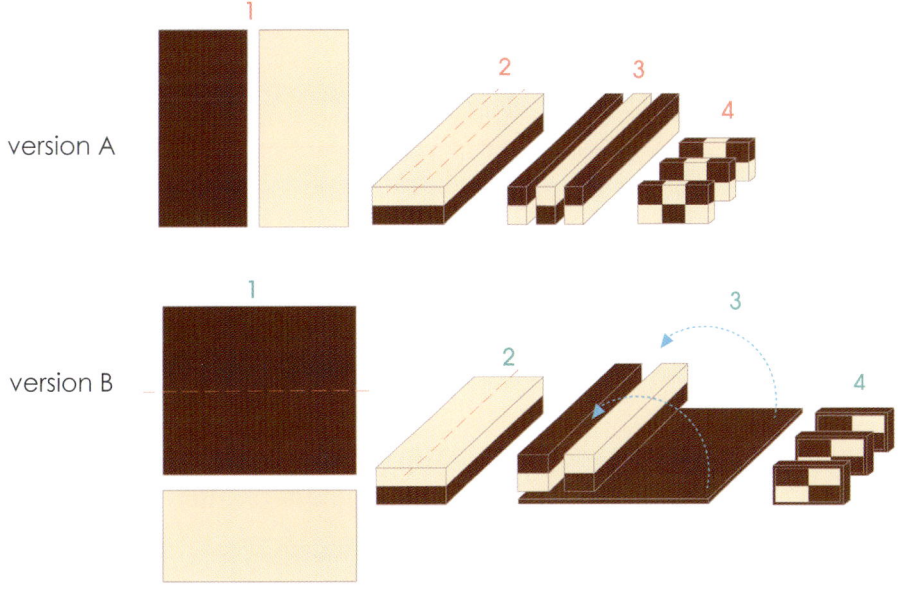

biscotti

120 g (4$^1/_3$ oz) unsalted butter

$^1/_2$ tsp salt

150 g (5$^1/_3$ oz) castor (superfine) sugar

275 g (9$^4/_5$ oz) plain (all-purpose) flour
+ 1 tsp baking powder, sifted

2 eggs

$^1/_2$ tsp vanilla extract or $^1/_4$ tsp ground vanilla

2 tsp orange zest

1 Tbsp orange juice

60 g (2$^1/_4$ oz) blanched walnuts or almonds,
chopped

150 g (5$^1/_3$ oz) raisins

100 g (3$^1/_2$ oz) candied mixed fruit

1 egg white for glazing

1 Tbsp sugar for sprinkling

- Preheat oven to 150°C (300°F). Line a baking tray with baking paper. Set aside.

- In a large mixing bowl, add butter, salt, sugar and flour and stir with a fork until mixture is grainy. Add eggs, vanilla, orange zest and orange juice. Mix and knead by hand until combined. Add nuts, raisins and candied fruits and knead again to combine.

- Divide mixture into 2 equal portions, and shape each portion into 9 x 2-cm (3$^1/_2$ x 1-in) rectangular block. Transfer blocks onto prepared tray. Brush surfaces of dough with egg white and sprinkle sugar on top.

- Place in preheated oven and bake for about 25 minutes until golden brown.

- Remove and leave to cool on a wire rack before slicing along breadth of each block into 1-cm ($^1/_2$-in) thick slices. Arrange sliced cookies on baking tray and return to oven at 140°C (280°F) for 3–5 minutes until cookies are dry.

- Remove and leave to cool before serving or storing in airtight containers.

ring**cookies**

100 g (3$^1/_2$ oz) butter + more for greasing

50 g (1$^2/_3$ oz) margarine

100 g (3$^1/_2$ oz) icing (confectioner's) sugar

$^1/_4$ tsp salt

1 egg yolk

2 Tbsp chopped, blanched almonds

250 g (9 oz) plain (all-purpose) flour

1 egg yolk for glazing

2 Tbsp sugar for sprinkling

- Preheat oven to 130°C (270°F). Line tray with baking paper and grease with butter. Set aside.

- With an electric mixer, beat sugar, butter and margarine until light and fluffy. Add salt and egg yolk and beat until well-combined. Add almonds and flour and stir with a fork or wooden spoon until combined and dough no longer feels sticky to touch.

- With a rolling pin, roll out dough to about 0.5-cm ($^1/_4$-in) thickness. Cut out cookies using a flower ring-shaped cookie cutter. Transfer to prepared baking tray. Glaze cookies with egg yolk and sprinkle sugar on top.

- Place in preheated oven and bake for about 30 minutes until cookies are done and golden brown. Leave to cool for 5 minutes before transferring to wire rack to cool completely.

- Remove and leave to cool before serving or storing in airtight containers.

butternutcookies

100 g (3^1/$_2$ oz) butter + more for greasing

50 g (1^2/$_3$ oz) margarine

1 egg

100 g (3^1/$_2$ oz) icing (confectioner's) sugar

100 g (3^1/$_2$ oz) grated palm sugar

^{1}/$_4$ tsp salt

150 g (5^1/$_3$ oz) peanut butter

275 g (9^4/$_5$ oz) plain (all-purpose) flour +
^{1}/$_4$ tsp baking powder + ^{1}/$_4$ tsp bicarbonate
of soda, sifted

3 Tbsp blanched, dry-roasted peanuts,
finely chopped

- Preheat oven to 140°C (280°F). Grease a baking tray with butter. Line tray with baking paper and grease again. Set aside.

- With an electric mixer, beat butter, margarine, egg and both types of sugar until light and fluffy. Add salt and peanut butter and beat until well-combined. Add flour mixture and stir with a fork or wooden spoon until combined and dough no longer feels sticky to touch.

- With a rolling pin, roll out dough to about 0.5-cm (^{1}/$_4$-in) thickness. Cut out cookie shapes with a cookie cutter of choice. Transfer to prepared baking tray. Sprinkle chopped peanuts on top of each cookie.

- Place in preheated oven and bake for about 20 minutes until cookies are done. Remove and leave to cool before serving or storing in airtight containers.

crystal glass cookies

150 g (5 1/3 oz) butter + more for greasing

60 g (2 1/4 oz) icing (confectioner's) sugar

1 egg

2 tsp orange zest

280 g (10 oz) plain (all-purpose) flour + 40 g (1 1/3 oz)
corn flour (cornstarch) + 1/2 tsp baking powder, sifted

1 tin fruit-flavoured crystal candies, unwrapped and
grouped according to colour

1 egg yolk for glazing

- Preheat oven to 180°C (350°F) for about 10 minutes before baking cookies. Grease a baking tray with butter, then line with baking paper and grease again. Prepare a pair of cookie cutters that are of an identical shape but of different sizes. Set aside.

- With an electric mixer, beat butter and sugar until light and fluffy. Add egg and orange zest and beat to combine well. Add flour mixture and stir with a fork or wooden spoon until combined and dough no longer feels sticky to touch. Wrap dough in plastic wrap and refrigerate for 1 hour.

- Place candies into separate plastic bags according to colour. Cover a bag with a tea towel and crush candies into flakes with a rolling pin. Set aside and repeat with remaining bags of candies.

- Roll out chilled cookie dough to 0.3-cm (1/8-in) thickness between 2 sheets of plastic wrap or non-stick baking paper. Use the bigger cookie cutter to cut cookies out and the smaller one to cut out a hole in the centre of each cookie. Carefully transfer cookies to prepared tray and glaze with egg yolk.

- Place in oven and bake for about 20 minutes. Remove tray from oven and fill each cookie centre with flaked candies. Return to oven for 15–20 minutes until candy flakes have sufficiently melted to fill hole in centre of each cookie. If required, add more candy flakes to fill up any gaps, or level candy flakes with handle of a metal spoon greased with a little cooking oil.

- Remove tray from oven and leave to cool until candy centres have solidified. Remove cookies from tray with care as they are fragile and crumble easily.

peanut**butter**sandwich

100 g (3^1/$_2$ oz) butter + more for greasing

50 g (1^2/$_3$ oz) icing (confectioner's) sugar

1 egg yolk

^{1}/$_4$ tsp salt

175 g (6^1/$_4$ oz) plain (all-purpose) flour, sifted

4 Tbsp creamy peanut butter + 2 tsp icing (confectioner's) sugar, well mixed

1 egg yolk for glazing

- Preheat oven to 130°C (270°F). Grease a baking tray with butter. Line tray with baking paper and grease again. Set aside.

- With an electric mixer, beat butter and sugar until light and fluffy. Add egg yolk and salt and beat until well-combined. Add flour and stir with a fork or wooden spoon until combined and dough no longer feels sticky to touch.

- With a rolling pin, roll out dough to 0.3-cm (^{1}/$_8$-in) thickness. Using a 3-cm (1^1/$_4$-in) diameter round cookie cutter, cut out rounds of dough. Transfer to prepared tray.

- Place in preheated oven and bake for about 20 minutes until half-done.

- Remove tray from oven. Divide cookie rounds into 2 equal batches. Spread peanut butter mixture on 1 batch of cookies and sandwich with plain cookies.

- Arrange cookies on tray and glaze with egg yolk. Return to oven and bake until cookies are done and golden brown.

- Remove and leave to cool before serving or storing in airtight containers.

kaastengels

250 g (9 oz) butter

100 g (3 1/2 oz) margarine

4 egg yolks

1/2 tsp salt

200 g (7 oz) grated matured cheese (Edam)

600 g (1 lb 5 1/3 oz) plain (all-purpose) flour, sifted

2 egg yolks for glazing

50 g (1 2/3 oz) grated cheddar cheese

- Preheat oven to 160°C (325°F). Line tray with baking paper. Set aside.

- With an electric mixer, beat butter, margarine, egg yolks, and salt until light and fluffy. Add grated cheese and beat until well-combined. Add flour and stir with a fork or wooden spoon until combined and dough no longer feels sticky to touch.

- Divide dough into 2 or 3 equal portions. With a rolling pin, roll out each portion to a rectangular shape with thickness of 0.7-cm (1/4-in). Glaze surfaces of each rectangular-shaped dough with egg yolks. Sprinkle grated cheddar cheese on top. Cut into 1.5 x 4-cm (3/4 x 1 1/2-in) pieces. Transfer to prepared baking tray, leaving a 1-cm (1/2-in) gap between cookies.

- Bake in preheated oven for 15–20 minutes until cookies are done and golden brown. Remove and leave to cool before serving or storing in airtight containers.

gingerbread cookies

125 g (4$\frac{1}{2}$ oz) butter + more for greasing

2 Tbsp milk powder

100 g (3$\frac{1}{2}$ oz) grated palm sugar

25 g ($\frac{3}{4}$ oz) castor (superfine) sugar

$\frac{1}{4}$ tsp salt

1 egg

1 Tbsp grated ginger

1 tsp ground cinnamon

1 tsp ground cloves

360 g (12$\frac{1}{3}$ oz) plain (all-purpose) flour
+ $\frac{1}{2}$ tsp baking powder + $\frac{1}{2}$ tsp
bicarbonate of soda, sifted

Frosting

2 egg whites

500 g (1 lb 1$\frac{1}{2}$ oz) icing (confectioner's) sugar

Food colouring

- Preheat oven to 160°C (325°F). Grease a baking tray with butter. Line tray with baking paper and grease again. Set aside.

- With an electric mixer, beat butter or margarine, milk powder, both types of sugar and salt until light and fluffy. Add egg, ginger, cinnamon and cloves, and beat until well-combined. Add flour into the mixture and stir with a fork or wooden spoon until combined and dough no longer feels sticky to touch.

- With a rolling pin, roll out dough to 0.3-cm ($\frac{1}{8}$-in) thickness. Use a gingerbread man cookie cutter to cut out shapes. Transfer to prepared tray.

- Place in preheated oven and bake for 15–20 minutes until cookies are done. Press candies into dough for eyes while cookies are still warm.

- Prepare frosting. Beat egg whites until stiff peaks form. Gradually add icing sugar while whisking until combined. Tint separate portions of frosting with food colouring of choice. Place into piping bags fitted with tiny decorative tips and decorate cookies as desired.

biscuits with lemon icing

100 g (3^1/$_2$ oz) butter + more for greasing

2 Tbsp milk powder

100 g (3^1/$_2$ oz) castor (superfine) sugar

1 egg

215 g (7^2/$_3$ oz) plain flour + 2 Tbsp corn flour
(cornstarch), sifted

Icing

60 g (2^1/$_4$ oz) margarine, melted

225 g (8 oz) icing (confectioner's) sugar

1 Tbsp hot water

1 tsp lemon zest

^{1}/$_2$ tsp lemon essence

- Preheat oven to 140°C (280°F). Grease a baking tray with butter. Line tray with baking paper and grease again. Set aside.

- With an electric mixer, beat all ingredients except flour mixture until light and fluffy. Add flour mixture and stir with a fork or wooden spoon until combined and dough no longer feels sticky to touch.

- With a rolling pin, roll out dough to 0.3-cm (^{1}/$_8$-in) thickness. Cut out shapes using a cookie cutter of choice and transfer to prepared tray. Using a fork, lightly prick surface of each cookie twice.

- Place in preheated oven and bake for 15–20 minutes until cookies are done and slightly brown. Remove and place on wire rack and leave to cool.

- Prepare icing. Stir all ingredients together in a mixing bowl with a fork until well-combined.

- Assemble cookies. Spread lemon icing on a cookie, then sandwich it with another plain cookie. Repeat step until cookies and icing are used up. Serve or store in airtight containers.

funcookies

200 g (7 oz) butter + more for greasing

150 g (5^1/$_3$ oz) icing (confectioner's) sugar

1 egg

350 g (12 oz) plain (all-purpose) flour
+ ^{1}/$_4$ tsp baking powder, sifted

1 quantity sugar frosting (page 12)

- Preheat oven to 150°C (300°F) 10 minutes before baking. Line a baking tray with baking paper and grease with butter. Set aside.

- With an electric mixer, beat butter or margarine, sugar and egg until light and fluffy. Add flour mixture and stir with a fork or wooden spoon until combined and dough no longer feels sticky to touch.

- Place dough in a mixing bowl. Cover with a damp tea towel and set aside in a cool room for 30 minutes.

- Sprinkle work surface and rolling pin with a little flour. Roll out dough to 0.3-cm (^{1}/$_8$-in) thickness and cut out dough shapes with cookie cutters of choice. Transfer to prepared tray.

- Place in preheated oven and bake for 15–20 minutes until cookies are done and golden. When cool, decorate with icing as desired. Serve or store in airtight containers

lollypop**cookies**

100 g (3$^1/_2$ oz) unsalted butter

100 g (3$^1/_2$ oz) white butter

1 egg

150 g (5$^1/_3$ oz) castor (superfine) sugar

1 tsp salt

1 tsp vanilla extract or $^1/_4$ tsp ground vanilla

380 g (13$^2/_3$ oz) plain (all-purpose) flour, sifted

Special cookie, satay or ice cream sticks

1 quantity sugar frosting (page 12)

- Preheat oven to 150°C (300°F) 10 minutes before baking. Line tray with baking paper. Set aside.

- With an electric mixer, beat all ingredients, except vanilla and flour, until light and fluffy. Add flour and vanilla and stir with a fork or wooden spoon until combined.

- Wrap dough in plastic wrap and refrigerate for 30 minutes.

- With a rolling pin, roll out dough to 0.3-cm ($^1/_8$-in) thickness. Use a cookie cutter of choice to cut out dough shapes.

- Assemble lollipop cookies. Lightly press 1 end of a stick in the centre of a cookie and sandwich with another cookie to form a 'lollipop'. Press lightly around edges of sandwiched cookies to ensure stick is secure. Repeat step with remaining cookies. Arrange cookies on prepared baking tray.

- Place in preheated oven and bake for 30 minutes until cookies are done. Remove and leave to cool on a wire rack. Decorate with icing as desired.

NOTE:

Special sticks for cookies can be purchased from baking specialty shops. If using satay or ice cream sticks, soak in water for about 2 hours before using to prevent the sticks from cracking when baked.

flowercookies

90 g (3 1/4 oz) unsalted butter + more for greasing

60 g (2 1/4 oz) icing (confectioner's) sugar

1/4 tsp salt

1 egg yolk

130 g (4 2/3 oz) plain (all-purpose) flour, sifted

1 quantity sugar frosting (page 12)

- Preheat oven to 150°C (300°F). Grease a baking tray with butter. Line tray with baking paper and grease again. Set aside.

- With an electric mixer, beat butter, sugar and salt until light and fluffy. Add egg yolk and beat until well-combined. Add flour into the mixture and stir in flour with a fork or wooden spoon until combined. Wrap dough in plastic wrap and refrigerate for 30 minutes.

- With a rolling pin, roll out dough to 0.3-cm (1/8-in) thickness. Use a flower-shaped cookie cutter with diameter of 2.5-cm (1-in) to cut out dough shapes. Arrange on prepared tray.

- Place in preheated oven and bake for 15–20 minutes until cookies are done. Remove and leave on a wire rack to cool. Decorate with icing. Fit piping bags with star-shaped nozzles and pipe icing of different colours onto cookies.

spekulaas

180 g (6^1/$_2$ oz) butter, softened +
more for greasing

230 g (8^1/$_4$ oz) plain (all-purpose) flour

30 g (1 oz) rice flour

^{1}/$_4$ tsp ground cinnamon

^{1}/$_8$ tsp ground cloves

1 tsp vanilla extract or ^{1}/$_4$ tsp ground vanilla

^{1}/$_4$ tsp ground mixed spices

150 g (5^1/$_3$ oz) castor (superfine) sugar

150 g (5^1/$_3$ oz) grated palm sugar

^{1}/$_4$ tsp salt

50 g (1^2/$_3$ oz) blanched almonds,
coarsely chopped

- Preheat oven to 170°C (330°F). Grease a baking tray with butter. Line tray with baking paper and grease again. Set aside.

- Sift flour, cinnamon, cloves, vanilla and mixed spices together into a mixing bowl. Set aside.

- Mix all ingredients except flour mixture and almonds with a fork in a mixing bowl until ingredients are well-combined. Add flour mixture and stir with a fork or wooden spoon until combined and dough no longer feels sticky to touch. Finally, mix in almonds.

- Prepare spekulaas moulds. Making sure they are clean and dry, sprinkle moulds evenly with some flour. Remove excess flour by inverting moulds and tapping on them.

- Spoon dough mixture into moulds and press until level. Use a knife to scrape off excess dough and neaten edges. Flip and tap each mould gently to loosen and release moulded dough shapes onto prepared baking tray.

- Place in preheated oven and bake for about 15 minutes until cookies are done and brown. Remove and leave to cool before serving or storing in airtight containers.

cashewnutcookies

150 g (5$^1/_3$ oz) butter + more for greasing

125 g (4$^1/_2$ oz) castor (superfine) sugar

2 tsp instant coffee granules, dissolved in
2 Tbsp hot water

$^1/_4$ tsp salt

1 tsp vanilla extract

225 g (8 oz) plain (all-purpose) flour
+ $^1/_2$ tsp bicarbonate of soda, sifted

150 g (5$^1/_3$ oz) dry-roasted cashew nuts;
100 g (3$^1/_2$ oz) coarsely chopped and
50 g (1$^2/_3$ oz) halved

- Preheat oven to 160°C (325°F). Grease a baking tray with butter. Set aside.

- With an electric mixer, beat butter, sugar, coffee mixture, salt and vanilla extract until light and combined. Add flour mixture and stir with a fork or wooden spoon until combined, then add chopped cashew nuts, and stir until mixture has combined to form a lump of soft dough.

- Pinch small amounts of dough and roll into 2.5-cm (1-in) balls. Arrange dough balls on prepared baking tray and flatten dough balls slightly. Press cashew halves on top of each cookie.

- Place in preheated oven and bake for about 20 minutes until cookies are done and golden brown.

- Remove and leave to cool before serving or storing in airtight containers.

special**date**cookies

200 g (7 oz) butter + more for greasing

$1/2$ tsp salt

1 tsp lemon extract or $1/2$ tsp lemon zest

1 tsp rose essence

50 g ($1^{2}/_{3}$ oz) castor (superfine) sugar

$2^{2}/_{3}$ Tbsp whipping cream or $1^{2}/_{3}$ Tbsp milk

1 egg

300 g (11 oz) plain (all-purpose) flour
+ 2 Tbsp rice flour

Icing (confectioner's) sugar

Filling

175 g ($6^{1}/_{4}$ oz) premium quality dates, pitted and chopped

50 ml ($1^{2}/_{3}$ fl oz) water

1 Tbsp sugar

$1/8$ tsp salt

100 g ($3^{1}/_{2}$ oz) walnuts or pecans, roasted and chopped

- Preheat oven to 140°C (280°F) 10 minutes before baking cookies. Line 1 baking tray with baking paper and grease another with butter. Set aside.

- Prepare filling. In a medium-size pot, stir all ingredients except nuts over low heat until dates have disintegrated. Leave to cool to room temperature. When cool, add chopped nuts of choice and stir to mix well. Scoop up $1/4$ tsp date mixture, then roll into a ball and set aside on greased baking tray. Repeat until date mixture is used up.

- Prepare cookie dough. With an electric mixer, beat all ingredients, except egg and flour mixture, until light and fluffy. Add egg and beat until well-combined. Add flour mixture and stir with a fork until combined and dough no longer feels sticky to touch.

- Taking 1 tsp cookie dough, roll it into a ball. Flatten into a round, then top with a ball of date mixture. Gather dough to enclose filling by using your fingers to gently stretch it over filling. Seal, then roll between hands to obtain a smooth ball or oval-shaped cookie. Flatten base slightly and place on prepared tray. Repeat until cookie and date mixtures are used up.

- Place in preheated oven and bake for about 40 minutes until done and golden brown. Remove and leave to cool on a wire rack. When cookies are completely cool, roll and coat them with icing sugar before serving.

sweetpretzels

160 g (5³/₄ oz) butter + more for greasing

70 g (2¹/₂ oz) icing (confectioner's) sugar

1 egg yolk

¹/₄ tsp vanilla extract

¹/₂ tsp orange zest

260 g (9¹/₃ oz) plain (all-purpose) flour + 1 tsp baking powder + ¹/₂ tsp milk powder, sifted

1 egg yolk for glazing

Sugar for sprinkling

- Preheat oven to 175°C (340°F) 15 minutes before baking. Grease a baking tray with butter. Set aside.

- With an electric mixer, beat butter, sugar, egg yolk, vanilla extract, and orange zest until light and fluffy. Add flour mixture and stir with a wooden spoon until combined. Cover with plastic wrap and chill mixture in fridge for 60 minutes.

- Remove mixture from fridge. Divide mixtures into 3 equal portions. Roll a portion of mixture into a long rope about 0.8-cm (¹/₃-in) thick, then cut into 9-cm (3¹/₂-in) lengths.

- Repeat with remaining 2 portions of mixture. To make a pretzel, gently bend 1 end of pastry length inwards to form a loop, then bring other end of pastry over first loop to form a pretzel shape. Place on prepared baking tray. Repeat until mixture is used up. Glaze pretzels with egg yolk and sprinkle sugar on top.

- Place in preheated oven and bake for 15–20 minutes until pretzels are done and golden.

- Remove and leave to cool before serving or storing in airtight containers.

peanutsesamecrunch

200 g (7 oz) butter + more for greasing + 50 g (1²/₃ oz) white butter

220 g (8 oz) castor (superfine) sugar

¹/₂ tsp salt

¹/₂ tsp vanilla extract

140 g (5 oz) dry-roasted peanuts, coarsely ground

50 g (1²/₃ oz) white sesame seeds, coarsely ground

280 g (10 oz) plain (all-purpose) flour + 1 tsp baking powder + 60 g (2¹/₄ oz) corn flour (cornstarch), sifted

White sesame seeds for coating

- Preheat oven to 180°C (350°F). Grease a baking tray with butter and set aside.

- With an electric mixer, beat butter, sugar, salt and vanilla extract until light and fluffy. Add ground peanuts and sesame seeds and stir with a wooden spoon until ingredients are combined. Add flour mixture and stir with a wooden spoon until combined.

- Taking 1 tsp cookie dough, roll it into a ball and coat with sesame seeds. Flatten into a 0.4-cm (1³/₄-in) round and place on prepared baking tray. Repeat until mixture is used up.

- Place in preheated oven and bake for 15–20 minutes until cookies are done.

- Remove and leave to cool before serving or storing in airtight containers.

snowwhite

140 g (5 oz) butter + more for greasing

75 g (2²/₃ oz) icing (confectioner's) sugar

2 egg yolks

¹/₄ tsp vanilla extract

170 g (6 oz) plain (all-purpose) flour, sifted

80 g (2⁴/₅ oz) dry-roasted cashew nuts, ground

Icing (confectioner's) sugar for coating

- Preheat oven to 180°C (350°F). Grease a baking tray with butter. Set aside.
- With an electric mixer, beat butter, sugar, egg yolks and vanilla extract until light and fluffy. Add flour and ground cashew nuts and stir with a wooden spoon until mixture has combined to form a lump of soft dough.
- Taking 1 tsp cookie dough, mould it into a crescent shape. Place on prepared baking tray. Repeat until dough is used up.
- Place in preheated oven and bake for 15–20 minutes until cookies are done and golden brown. Transfer to a wire rack and leave to cool before coating with icing sugar.

pinda**cookies**

100 g (3 $^1/_2$ oz) butter + more for greasing

75 g (2 $^2/_3$ oz) creamy peanut butter

100 g (3 $^1/_2$ oz) icing (confectioner's) sugar

100 g (3 $^1/_2$ oz) grated palm sugar

1 egg yolk

$^1/_2$ tsp vanilla extract

200 g (7 oz) plain (all-purpose) flour + 25 g ($^3/_4$ oz) corn flour (cornstarch) + $^1/_2$ tsp baking powder + $^1/_2$ tsp bicarbonate of soda, sifted

50 g (1 $^2/_3$ oz) dry-roasted, blanched peanuts or chocolate chips for decorating

- Preheat oven to 160°C (325°F). Grease a baking tray with butter. Set aside.

- With an electric mixer, beat butter, peanut butter, sugar, palm sugar, egg yolk and vanilla until light and fluffy. Add flour mixture and stir with a wooden spoon until mixture has combined to form a soft dough.

- Taking 1 tsp cookie dough, roll it into a ball, then flatten and place on prepared baking tray. Repeat until dough is used up. To decorate, press a peanut or chocolate chip into centre of each dough circle.

- Place in preheated oven and bake for about 20 minutes until cookies are done. Remove and leave to cool on a wire rack before serving or storing in airtight containers.

strawberrycookies

Butter for greasing

225 g (8 oz) plain (all-purpose) flour +
1$\frac{1}{2}$ Tbsp rice flour, sifted

50 g (1$\frac{2}{3}$ oz) icing (confectioner's) sugar

2 Tbsp dry-roasted cashew nuts, finely chopped

1 tsp vanilla extract

180 g (6$\frac{1}{2}$ oz) butter, whisked

50 g (1$\frac{2}{3}$ oz) strawberry jam, strained

30 g (1 oz) flaked almonds or dry-roasted
cashew nuts

- Preheat oven to 160°C (325°F). Grease a baking tray with butter. Set aside.

- In a large mixing bowl, combine flour mixture, sugar, cashew nuts and vanilla extract with a wooden spoon. Add butter and stir with a fork until mixture has combined to form a soft dough.

- Taking 1 tsp mixture, roll it into a ball. Flatten and place on prepared baking tray. Repeat until dough is used up. Leave a gap between cookies on baking tray. Using the tip of a chopstick, make an indentation in the centre of each cookie and fill with strawberry jam. Top each cookie with an almond flake or cashew nut.

- Place in preheated oven and bake for about 20 minutes until cookies are done and golden brown.

- Remove and leave to cool before serving or storing in airtight containers.

pineapple**balls**

Filling

1 medium pineapple, peeled and grated

75 g (2²/₃ oz) castor (superfine) sugar

2 cloves

5-cm (2-in) cinnamon stick

Pastry

200 g (7 oz) butter + more for greasing

3 Tbsp grated matured cheese (Edam or Gouda)

50 g (1²/₃ oz) icing (confectioner's) sugar

1 Tbsp milk powder

3 egg yolks

250 g (9 oz) plain (all-purpose) flour
+ 25 g (³/₄ oz) corn flour (cornstarch), sifted

2 egg yolks for glazing

- Preheat oven to 120°C (250°F) 10 minutes before baking. Grease a baking tray with butter. Set aside.

- Prepare filling. In a medium-size pot, cook pineapple over medium heat until juice has evaporated completely. Add sugar, cloves and cinnamon stick. Stirring constantly, cook pineapple mixture until it turns dark brown and is the consistency of thick jam. Remove and leave to cool to room temperature.

- Prepare pastry. With an electric mixer, beat all ingredients (except flour mixture) until light and fluffy. Add flour mixture and stir with a fork until combined and dough no longer feels sticky to touch.

- Assemble pineapple balls. Spoon 2 tsp pastry mixture and roll into a ball, then flatten into a round. Top with 1 tsp pineapple jam. Gather dough to enclose filling and seal. Roll between hands to obtain a smooth ball. Flatten base slightly and place on prepared baking tray. Repeat with remaining pastry and filling until ingredients are finished. Leave a gap between pineapple balls when arranging on tray.

- Place in preheated oven and bake for about 30 minutes until pineapple balls are done. Remove and glaze with beaten egg yolks. Return to oven and bake again until pineapple balls are golden brown. Transfer to a wire rack and leave to cool before serving.

caramelsticks

250 g (9 oz) butter + more for greasing

100 g (3$^1/_2$ oz) icing (confectioner's) sugar

2 egg yolks

$^1/_2$ tsp vanilla extract

300 g (11 oz) plain (all-purpose) flour +
25 g ($^3/_4$ oz) corn flour (cornstarch), sifted

Decoration

250 g (9 oz) castor (superfine) sugar

200 g (7 oz) dry-roasted, blanched peanuts, chopped

- Preheat oven to 150°C (300°F). Grease a baking tray with butter. Set aside.

- With an electric mixer, beat all ingredients (except flour mixture) until light and fluffy. Add flour mixture and stir with a fork until well-combined. Transfer mixture to a piping bag attached with a serrated nozzle, or to a disposable piping bag. If using disposable piping bag, cut tip of bag to make a 1-cm ($^1/_2$-in) diameter round hole.

- Pipe pastry mixture in 5-cm (2-in) lengths in the shape of the letter 'U' onto prepared baking tray.

- Place in preheated oven and bake for about 20 minutes or until cookies are brown.

- Prepare decoration. In a medium-size pot, cook sugar over low heat until completely dissolved and caramelised. Dip both ends of a cookie into sugar syrup and immediately coat with chopped peanuts. Leave to set on a wire rack. Repeat until all cookies have been dipped and coated. This step has to be executed quickly as sugar syrup hardens very quickly while it cools.

durianthorns

Filling

300 g (11 oz) durian flesh

100 g (3¹/₂ oz) grated palm sugar

Pastry

200 g (7 oz) butter + more for greasing

50 g (1 oz) icing (confectioner's) sugar

2 egg yolks

275 g (9⁴/₅ oz) plain (all-purpose) flour, sifted

1 egg yolk for glazing

- Preheat oven to 150°C (300°F) 10 minutes before baking. Grease a baking tray with butter. Set aside.

- Prepare filling. In a medium-size pot, cook all ingredients together over a low heat, stirring constantly until mixture has thickened into a paste that can be moulded. Remove and leave to cool to room temperature. When cool, spoon and roll 1 tsp durian paste into a ball and placed on a lightly greased tray. Repeat until durian paste is finished.

- Prepare pastry. With an electric mixer, beat all ingredients except flour until light and fluffy. Add flour mixture and stir with a fork until combined and dough no longer feels sticky to touch.

- Assemble durian cookies. Spoon 1 Tbsp pastry mixture and roll into a ball. Flatten into a round and top with a ball of durian paste. Gather dough to enclose filling and seal. Roll and mould with hands to obtain an oblong shape. Flatten base slightly and place on prepared baking tray. Repeat with remaining pastry and filling until ingredients are finished. When cookies have been made, cut surfaces of cookies with a pair of kitchen scissors so that cookies resemble durians with thorns. Glaze cookies with beaten egg yolk.

- Place in preheated oven and bake for about 50 minutes until cookies are done and golden brown.

- Remove and leave to cool before serving or storing in airtight containers.

almondflakecookies

250 g (9 oz) butter

$^1/_2$ tsp vanilla extract

200 g (7 oz) icing (confectioner's) sugar

180 ml (6 fl oz / $^3/_4$ cup) egg whites

225 g (8 oz) plain (all-purpose) flour +
25 g ($^3/_4$ oz) cocoa powder, sifted

75 g (2$^2/_3$ oz) almond flakes

- Preheat oven to 180ºC (350ºF). Line a baking tray, then place in the fridge to chill.

- With an electric mixer, beat butter, ground vanilla and sugar until light and fluffy. While beating constantly, add egg whites gradually until combined. Continue to beat and add flour mixture in small batches until ingredients are combined. Transfer mixture to a disposable piping bag and cut tip of bag to make a 1-cm ($^1/_2$-in) diameter round hole.

- Pipe mixture to form 3-cm (1$^1/_4$-in) diameter rounds onto chilled tray. Sprinkle almond flakes on top.

- Place in preheated oven and bake for about 15 minutes until cookies are done.

- Remove and leave to cool before serving or storing in airtight containers.

ladyfingers

3 eggs, yolks and whites separated

80 g (2^4/$_5$ oz) castor (superfine) sugar

70 g (2^1/$_3$ oz) plain (all-purpose) flour +
20 g (^{2}/$_3$ oz) corn flour (cornstarch), sifted

- Preheat oven to 180°C (350°F). Line a baking tray, then place in the fridge to chill.

- With an electric mixer, beat egg yolks with 10 g (^{1}/$_3$ oz) sugar until mixture is thick and pale. Set aside. Using clean beaters and in a clean and dry bowl, beat egg whites with remaining 70 g (2^1/$_2$ oz) sugar until stiff peaks form.

- Using a wooden spoon or rubber spatula, gradually fold egg white mixture in small batches into yolk mixture until well-combined. Gently fold flour mixture in small batches into egg mixture until combined.

- Transfer mixture to a piping bag and cut to make a 2^1/$_2$-cm (1-in) hole. Pipe mixture in 8-cm (3-in) lengths onto prepared tray.

- Place in preheated oven and bake for about 10 minutes until cookies are done. Remove tray from oven, then lower oven temperature to 130°C (260°F) and leave for 20 minutes before returning cookies to oven. Bake for about 20 minutes until cookies are crisp.

- Remove and leave to cool before serving or storing in airtight containers.

cat'stonguecookies

250 g (9 oz) butter

200 g (7 oz) icing (confectioner's) sugar

180 ml (6 fl oz / $^3/_4$ cup) egg whites

$^1/_2$ tsp vanilla extract

250 g (9 oz) plain (all-purpose) flour, sifted

- Preheat oven to 180°C (350°F). Line a baking tray, then place in the fridge to chill.

- With an electric mixer, beat all ingredients except flour until light and fluffy. Whisking constantly, add flour in small batches until ingredients are well combined. Transfer mixture to a disposable piping bag and cut tip of bag to make a 1-cm ($^1/_2$-in) diameter round hole.

- Pipe mixture to form 5-cm (2-in) lengths onto chilled tray.

- Place in preheated oven and bake for 12–15 minutes until cookies have expanded sideways and are brown around the edges.

- Remove and leave to cool before serving or storing in airtight containers.

cheese sago cookies

100 g (3^1/$_2$ oz) butter + more for greasing

150 g (5^1/$_3$ oz) margarine

225 g (8 oz) icing (confectioner's) sugar

2 egg yolks

100 g (3^1/$_2$ oz) matured cheese (Edam), grated
+ 100 g (3^1/$_2$ oz cheddar cheese, grated and
left to air-dry

425 g (15^1/$_4$ oz) sago flour, sifted

- Preheat oven to 150°C (300°F). Grease a baking tray with butter. Set aside.

- With an electric mixer, beat butter, margarine, sugar and egg yolks until light and fluffy. Add cheese and stir to combine well. Divide mixture and sago flour into 4 equal portions.

- In another mixing bowl, add a portion of cheese mixture and a portion of sago flour and mix lightly. Transfer to a piping bag fitted with nozzle of choice. Pipe mixture in ring shapes or other shapes as desired onto prepared tray.

- Repeat step above with remaining portions of cheese mixture and flour until all ingredients are used up.

- Place in preheated oven and bake for about for 20 minutes until cookies are done. Transfer to a wire rack and leave to cool completely before storing in an airtight container.

NOTE:

The cheese mixture and sago flour are mixed in small batches to keep the mixture aerated for lighter cookies.

cocococrunchwhistles

250 g (9 oz) butter + more for greasing

175 g (6 1/4 oz) icing (confectioner's) sugar

1 egg yolk

1/2 tsp instant coffee granules

250 g (9 oz) plain (all-purpose) flour
+ 20 g (2/3 oz) cocoa powder, sifted

25 g (3/4 oz) chocolate-flavoured cereal
for decorating

- Preheat oven to 130°C (270°F). Grease a baking tray with butter. Set aside.

- With an electric mixer, beat all ingredients, except flour mixture and cereal until light and fluffy. Add flour mixture and stir with a wooden spoon until well-combined. Transfer mixture to a piping bag fitted with a star-shaped or flower-shaped nozzle.

- Pipe mixture onto prepared tray. Leave a gap between cookies. Top each cookie with some cereal.

- Place in preheated oven and bake for about 25 minutes until cookies are done. Remove and leave to cool before serving or storing in airtight containers.

coconutmacaroons

300 g (11 oz) butter + more for greasing

350 g (12 oz) icing (confectioner's) sugar

$^1/_2$ tsp salt

$^1/_2$ tsp vanilla extract

3 egg yolks

300 g (11 oz) plain (all-purpose) flour, sifted

$^1/_2$ coconut, grated and stir-fried without oil until dry

- Preheat oven to 150°C (300°F). Grease a baking tray with butter. Set aside.

- With an electric mixer, beat butter, sugar, salt and vanilla extract until light and fluffy. Add egg yolks and beat until combined. Use a wooden spoon to gradually fold flour and grated coconut in small amounts into butter mixture, mixing well at each turn.

- Drop 1 tsp cookie dough onto prepared tray. Flatten each portion with the back of a fork to create grooves on surface of cookie. Repeat until dough is used up. Leave a gap between cookies on tray.

- Place in preheated oven and bake for 25 minutes until cookies are done and golden brown. Transfer to a wire rack and leave to cool before serving or storing in airtight containers.

balinese**chocolate** **nut**cookies

200 g (7 oz) butter + more for greasing

150 g (5 $^1/_3$ oz) castor (superfine) sugar

1 egg

75 g (2 $^2/_3$ oz) cooking chocolate, melted and cooled

250 g (9 oz) plain (all-purpose) flour + 1 tsp baking powder, sifted

150 g (5 $^1/_3$ oz) dry, salted peanuts or salted blanched peanuts, coarsely chopped

- Preheat oven to 130°C (270°F). Grease a baking tray with butter. Set aside.

- With an electric mixer, beat butter, sugar and egg until light and fluffy. Add melted chocolate and beat to combine well. Add flour mixture and stir with a fork until combined, then add nuts and stir until combined.

- Drop 1 tsp cookie dough onto prepared tray. Repeat until dough is used up. Leave a gap between cookies on tray.

- Place in preheated oven and bake for about 25 minutes until cookies are done. Transfer to a wire rack and leave to cool before serving or storing in airtight containers.

chocolate cashew schuimpjes

125 ml (4 fl oz / $1/2$ cup) egg white (about 4 eggs)

250 g (9 oz) castor (superfine) sugar

200 g (7 oz) dry-roasted cashew nuts, coarsely chopped

100 g (3$1/2$ oz) dark cooking chocolate, grated and kept in fridge to chill

- Preheat oven to 130°C (270°F). Line a baking tray with baking paper. Set aside.

- With an electric mixer, beat egg whites at low speed until foamy. Gradually add sugar and continue to beat until sugar has dissolved completely. Increase mixer speed and beat for about 10 minutes until stiff peaks form. Add cashew nuts and chilled grated chocolate. Gently fold mixture with a wooden spoon until just combined.

- Drop 1 tsp cookie dough onto prepared tray and repeat until used up. Leave a gap between cookies on tray.

- Place in preheated oven and bake for about 50 minutes until cookies are done and slightly golden. Transfer to a wire rack and leave to cool. After the cookies have cooled, store them in an airtight container immediately to prevent them from losing their crunch.

snow**coffee**cookies

300 g (11 oz) butter + more for greasing

180 g (6^1/$_2$ oz) castor (superfine) sugar

1^1/$_2$ Tbsp instant coffee powder, dissolved in
1 Tbsp hot water

1 tsp vanilla extract

^{1}/$_2$ tsp salt

450 g (1 lb) plain (all-purpose) flour
+ ^{1}/$_2$ tsp bicarbonate of soda, sifted

200 g (7 oz) dry-roasted cashew nuts, chopped

200 g (7 oz) icing (confectioner's) sugar for dusting

- Preheat oven to 130°C (270°F). Grease a baking tray with butter. Set aside.

- With an electric mixer, beat all ingredients except flour mixture, cashew nuts and icing sugar, until light and fluffy. Add flour mixture and stir with a fork or wooden spoon until combined. Add cashew nuts and stir until ingredients are combined.

- Spoon 1 tsp mixture and shape into a ball with the aid of another teaspoon. Transfer to prepared tray and repeat with remaining mixture until finished. Leave a gap between cookies on tray. Flatten each cookie slightly by pressing down with the back of a fork.

- Place in preheated oven and bake for 20–30 minutes until cookies are done. Transfer cookies to a wire rack and leave to cool completely. Dust with icing sugar before serving.

chocolate chip cookies

200 g (7 oz) butter + more for greasing

200 g (7 oz) brown sugar or grated palm sugar

100 g (3¹/₂ oz) castor (superfine) sugar

¹/₂ tsp salt

¹/₂ tsp vanilla extract

2 egg whites

400 g (14¹/₃ oz) plain (all-purpose) flour + 1 tsp
baking powder, sifted

250 g (9 oz) chocolate chips or cooking chocolate,
chopped

150 g (5¹/₃ oz) dry-roasted cashew nuts, chopped

- Preheat oven to 130°C (270°F). Grease a baking tray with butter. Set aside.

- With an electric mixer, beat butter, brown or palm sugar, castor sugar, salt and vanilla extract until mixture is thick and pale. While beating constantly, add egg whites one by one until mixture is just combined. Add flour mixture and stir with a wooden spoon until just combined. Finally, add chocolate and cashew nuts and stir until ingredients are well-combined.

- Drop teaspoonfuls of mixture onto prepared tray, then flatten each cookie slightly by pressing down with the back of a teaspoon. Leave a gap between cookies.

- Place in preheated oven and bake for about 25 minutes until cookies are done. Remove and leave to cool on a wire rack before serving or storing in airtight containers.

dried**fruit**cookies

50 g (1^2/$_3$ oz) butter, softened + more for greasing

50 g (1^2/$_3$ oz) margarine, softened

150 g (5^1/$_3$ oz) castor (superfine) sugar

^{1}/$_2$ tsp vanilla extract

^{1}/$_4$ tsp salt

^{1}/$_2$ tsp orange zest

225 g (8 oz) plain (all-purpose) flour + ^{1}/$_2$ tsp
bicarbonate of soda + 1 tsp baking powder, sifted

1 Tbsp milk

1^1/$_2$ eggs, lightly beaten

100 g (3^1/$_2$ oz) raisins, halved

100 g (3^1/$_2$ oz) dry-roasted cashew nuts, chopped

Decoration

10 glacé red cherries, cut into small pieces

50 g (1^2/$_3$ oz) almond flakes

- Preheat oven to 140°C (280°F). Grease a baking tray with butter. Line with baking paper and grease again. Set aside.

- In a large mixing bowl, add butter, margarine, sugar, vanilla extract, salt and orange zest and stir with a fork until combined. Add flour mixture and stir with a fork until mixture is grainy. Add milk and eggs and stir again until mixture is combined. Add raisins and cashew nuts and stir until well-combined.

- Drop teaspoonfuls of cookie dough onto prepared tray. Flatten each cookie slightly by pressing down with the back of a teaspoon. Leave a gap between cookies on tray. Top each cookie with some cherries and almond flakes.

- Place in preheated oven and bake for about 25 minutes until cookies are done and golden brown. Leave cookies to cool completely before peeling them off the baking paper as they tend to stick when hot.

lacecookies

75 g (2²/₃ oz) unsalted butter, melted + more for greasing

115 g (4 oz) brown sugar or grated palm sugar

¹/₈ tsp salt

1 egg white

¹/₂ tsp ground mixed spices

2 tsp plain (all-purpose) flour

1 tsp baking powder

75 g (2²/₃ oz) oatmeal

50 g (1²/₃ oz) raisins or glacé cherries, finely chopped

- Preheat oven to 160°C (325°F). Grease a baking tray with butter. Line with non-stick baking paper. Using a 6-cm (2¹/₂-in) diameter round cookie cutter, draw circles on baking paper. Grease circles with butter. Set aside.

- In a large mixing bowl, add all ingredients except raisins or cherries, and stir with a wooden spoon until ingredients are combined.

- Drop 1 tsp mixture in the centre of a traced circle on prepared tray and spread evenly to fill circle. Sprinkle some chopped raisins or cherries on top. Repeat until mixture is used up.

- Place in preheated oven and bake for 7 minutes or until brown. Lift baking paper with cookies onto a wire rack to cool completely before peeling them off baking paper. The cookies tend to stick when hot. Serve or store in airtight containers.

NOTE:

Use non-stick baking paper when baking cookies with high sugar content such as lace cookies, as the cookies tend to stick on regular baking paper and will be difficult to remove.

peanut**chunk**cookies

Butter for greasing

2 egg yolks

150 g (5$^1/_3$ oz) grated palm sugar

$^1/_2$ tsp salt

150 g (5$^1/_2$ oz) dry-roasted, blanched peanuts,
coarsely chopped

$^1/_4$ tsp ground ginger or $^1/_4$ tsp fresh ginger juice

1 egg white

$^1/_8$ tsp salt

75 g (2$^2/_3$ oz) plain (all-purpose) flour, sifted

- Preheat oven to 160°C (325°F). Grease a baking tray with butter. Line with non-stick baking paper. Set aside.

- With an electric mixer, beat egg yolks until mixture is pale and thick. While beating constantly, add palm sugar in small batches followed by $^1/_2$ tsp salt until combined. Add peanuts and ground ginger or ginger juice and stir to combine the ingredients well.

- In a separate bowl, beat egg white with salt until stiff peaks form. Using a rubber spatula or wooden spoon, fold egg white into peanut mixture until combined. Lastly, fold in flour until ingredients are combined.

- Drop teaspoonfuls of mixture onto prepared tray, leaving a 3-cm (1$^1/_4$-in) gap between cookies. Repeat until mixture is finished.

- Place in preheated oven and bake for 15–20 minutes until cookies are done.

- Remove and leave to cool before serving or storing in airtight containers.

bananachipcookies

200 g (7 oz) butter + more for greasing

150 g (5$^1/_3$ oz) castor (superfine) sugar

$^1/_8$ tsp salt

1 egg yolk + $^1/_2$ egg white

1 tsp banana essence

200 g (7 oz) plain (all-purpose) flour, sifted

200 g (7 oz) sweet banana chips, crumbed

- Preheat oven to 120°C (250°F). Grease a baking tray with butter.

- With an electric mixer, beat all ingredients (except flour and banana chips) until mixture is creamy. Using a rubber spatula or wooden spoon, fold in flour and banana chips in small batches respectively until combined.

- Drop teaspoonfuls of cookie dough onto prepared tray. Flatten each cookie slightly by pressing down with the back of a teaspoon. Keep cookies slightly apart.

- Place in preheated oven and bake for about 20 minutes or until cookies are golden brown. Transfer to a wire rack and leave to cool before serving or storing in airtight containers.

cornflake meringues

Butter for greasing

4 egg whites

200 g (7 oz) castor (superfine) sugar

100 g (3^1/$_2$ oz) dry-roasted cashew nuts, chopped

^{1}/$_4$ coconut, shell discarded and flesh removed, grated and stir-fried without oil until dry

75 g (2^2/$_3$ oz) cornflakes, crumbed

75 g (2^2/$_3$ oz) plain (all-purpose) flour, sifted

- Preheat oven to 100°C (200°F). Grease a baking tray with butter. Line with baking paper. Set aside.

- With an electric mixer, beat egg whites until stiff peaks form. While beating constantly, add sugar in small batches and beat until stiff peaks form. Using a wooden spoon, gently fold cashew nuts, coconut, cornflakes and flour into egg white mixture until ingredients are combined.

- Drop teaspoonfuls of cookie dough onto prepared tray. Leave a gap between cookies.

- Place in preheated oven and bake for about 50 minutes until cookies are done. Remove and leave to cool before serving or storing in airtight containers.

cashewoatmealcookies

250 g (9 oz) butter + more for greasing

200 g (7 oz) brown sugar or grated palm sugar

110 g (4 oz) castor (superfine) sugar

$^1/_2$ tsp salt

2 egg yolks + 1 egg white

$^1/_2$ tsp vanilla extract

200 g (7 oz) plain (all-purpose) flour + $^1/_2$ tsp
bicarbonate of soda, sifted

200 g (7 oz) oatmeal

200 g (7 oz) dry-roasted cashew nuts, chopped

- Preheat oven to 150°C (300°F). Grease a baking tray with butter. Set aside.

- With an electric mixer, beat all ingredients (except flour mixture, oatmeal and cashew nuts) until mixture is creamy. Add flour mixture and stir with a wooden spoon or fork until combined. Add oatmeal and cashew nuts and stir until combined.

- Drop teaspoonfuls of cookie dough onto prepared tray. Flatten each cookie slightly by pressing down with the back of a teaspoon. Leave a gap between cookies.

- Place in preheated oven and bake for about 20 minutes until cookies are done and golden brown. Transfer to a wire rack and leave to cool before serving or storing in airtight containers.

oatmeal**raisin**cookies

125 g (4^1/$_2$ oz) unsalted butter + more for greasing

200 g (7 oz) castor (superfine) sugar

^{1}/$_2$ tsp salt

1 egg

1 tsp vanilla extract

1 tsp orange zest

125 g (4^1/$_2$ oz) plain (all-purpose) flour + ^{1}/$_2$ tsp bicarbonate of soda + ^{1}/$_2$ tsp baking powder, sifted

160 g (5^3/$_4$ oz) oatmeal

125 g (4^1/$_2$ oz) raisins

- Preheat oven to 160°C (325°F). Grease a baking tray with butter. Set aside.

- With an electric mixer, beat butter, sugar and salt until mixture is light and fluffy. Add egg, vanilla extract and orange zest and beat until combined. Using a wooden spoon, fold flour mixture in small batches into butter mixture until combined. Lastly, fold in oatmeal and raisins until ingredients are combined.

- Drop teaspoonfuls of cookie dough onto prepared tray. Leave a gap between cookies.

- Place in preheated oven and bake for about 20 minutes until cookies are done and golden brown. Remove and leave to cool before serving or storing in airtight containers.

cornflake cookies

200 g (7 oz) butter + more for greasing

165 g (5 $^4/_5$ oz) castor (superfine) sugar

1 egg yolk + $^1/_2$ egg white

$^1/_2$ tsp lemon or vanilla extract

$^1/_4$ tsp salt

100 g (3 $^1/_2$ oz) plain (all-purpose) flour, sifted

100 g (3 $^1/_2$ oz) cornflakes

- Preheat oven to 120°C (250°F). Grease a baking tray with butter. Set aside.

- With an electric mixer, beat all ingredients (except flour and cornflakes) until mixture is creamy. Add flour and stir with a wooden spoon until combined. Add cornflakes and stir until combined.

- Drop teaspoonfuls of cookie dough onto prepared tray. Leave a gap between cookies.

- Place in preheated oven and bake for about 20 minutes until cookies are done and golden brown. Remove and leave to cool before serving or storing in airtight containers.

chewy**chocolate**cookies

200 g (7 oz) butter + more for greasing

150 g (5 $^1/_3$ oz) castor (superfine) sugar

$^1/_8$ tsp salt

1 egg white

$^1/_2$ tsp vanilla extract

250 g (9 oz) plain (all-purpose) flour + 1 tsp
baking powder, sifted

100 g (3 $^1/_2$ oz) raisins

100 g (3 $^1/_2$ oz) dry-roasted cashew nuts, chopped

75 g (2 $^2/_3$ oz) dark cooking chocolate, melted

- Preheat oven to 130°C (270°F). Grease a baking tray with butter. Set aside.

- With an electric mixer, beat butter, sugar, salt, egg white and vanilla extract until mixture is light and fluffy. Using a wooden spoon, fold in half the flour mixture, raisins and cashew nuts and stir until combined. Add melted chocolate and stir until combined. Fold in remaining flour mixture, raisins and cashew nuts until ingredients are well-combined.

- Drop tablespoonfuls of cookie dough onto prepared tray. Leave a 5-cm (2-in) gap between cookies.

- Place in preheated oven and bake for about 25 minutes until cookies are done. Transfer to a wire rack and leave to cool before serving or storing in airtight containers.

Yasa Boga, meaning "food maker" in Indonesian, is made up of a group of three homemakers who are also career women.

Hayatinufus A.L. Tobing, a former Coordinator of Culinary tests at a popular women's magazine, has spent twenty-five years in the culinary field. Her experiences range from teaching home economics in high schools and examining and creating new recipes to practising this art. Her experience and knowledge have contributed much to the high quality of this book.

Cherry Hadibroto, the founder of the Yasa Boga group, is responsible for the production quality of many cookbooks. An entrepreneur with many years of experience working for a women's magazine, she understands what people want from recipes and cookbooks, and meets those demands in this cookbook.

Nies Kartohadiprojo has the talent and experience of transforming all kinds of recipes into delicious dishes that look equally appetising. Since her retirement from a popular women's magazine, she now accepts special catering orders for parties and celebrations where her culinary powers are evident.